BAG IT UP

BAG IT UP

a stage play by

Franciscus Spaan

Title: BAG IT UP

Franciscus Spaan: text, ©, cover-design, art-work

ISBN: 978-3-9525561-0-8

Imprint: WIVH books

Information: postfs@proton.me

"The first time I died
Was in the arms of good friends of mine.
...
The next time I dedicate
My life's work to the friends I make"

(Kate Bush – All the love / The Dreaming)

BAG IT UP

a stage play in seven scenes
by Franciscus Spaan

the cast - larger parts first:

- <u>Pete</u> – naive, enthusiastic, human, unsure; later more aggressive
- <u>James</u>, who is also one of the <u>Cubes</u> (see below) – academic, shop-dusted, superficial, traditional
- <u>Chuck</u> – technical, financial, blunt; later more anxious
- <u>Pearl</u>, who is also <u>Ex</u> – shrew, angel, undefinable, unpredictable; Ex develops into Pearl, from negative to positive
- <u>Mediator</u>, who is also the <u>Butler</u> – slimy, all about appearances, no back-bone
  <u>Butler</u> – switching between too friendly and angry, complaining
- <u>Office-clerk</u> – willing but nervous, weak
- <u>System-manager</u> – digital, monotone, cold
- several additional <u>Cubes</u> – members of a square brotherhood trying to meditate
- a <u>Speaker</u>
  texts are from:
  - the Ship of Death by D. H. Lawrence
  - the Egyptian Book of the Dead
  - the author

SCENE 1

*Scene - an library-like interior, a desk, dusty
books and other objects*

*James - on stage, asleep among the books
Later Pete and Chuck*

*The poem is generally spoken with solemnity, in
contrast with what is going on on stage*

Speaker
*optionally walking through the audience, heralding
a grave message*

> Now it is autumn and the falling fruit
> and the long journey towards oblivion.
> The apples falling like great drops of dew
> to bruise themselves
> an exit from themselves.
> And it is time to go,
> to bid farewell to one's own self,
> and find an exit
> from the fallen self.

James starts snoring

> Have you built your ship of death,
> O have you?
> O build your ship of death,
> for you will need it.

Enter Pete - searching for something

Pete

> You don't mind if I go through your stuff, do
> you James?
> ... James?
> Are you sleeping again?
> Or still...?

You're no use – why don't you help me
searching?

...

You and your books...
What I'm looking for is certainly not in those
dust-collectors of yours

...

Or is it?
Perhaps it is...
starts to browse through the books until one falls
James
waking up, still dreamy
...State your name please...
Pete

My name?
It's me, me – have you forgotten who I am?

...

Have you?
James
gradually coming to his senses
O ... Pete ... sorry about that, do come in,
make yourself at home, how are you doing,
etcetera, etcetera...
Pete
wants to start a long monologue
Well ... now that you're asking...
but does not know what to say
I'm alright, I suppose.
Don't know really.
It's a bit of a thing, you know.
James
What on Earth are you talking about?
You sound a bit silly dear boy, if you don't
mind me saying so.

Pete
starts searching again, demonstrates searching
I'm in this mode, you see, in this mode...
James
looks at Pete who demonstrates his searching
No I don't.

...
What are you looking for?
Have you lost something?
Pete
Yeah, come and help me find it!
James
Find what?
Pete
stops searching, turns to James
My karma!
continues searching
James
speechless

...
Find your ...
What?
Pete
My karma.
I have lost my karma.
James
I say ...
I... I...
recapturing himself
I'm afraid I didn't quite get what you were
saying - do speak clearly dear boy - you've
lost ... ?
Pete
loud and clear
My karma!
I have lost my karma - I can't find it.

James
getting up, starting a lecture
>Pete, now let me explain this to you:
>One does not loose ones karma.

Pete
self-righteous
>Why not?

James
confused
>Eh... stop asking such silly questions.

hesitates, tries to find a book with the answer
>One doesn't ...because one...well...so...it...

closes books, proclaims:
>Tradition.
>It is tradition.

Pete
>Tradition!?
>O come on...

James
lecturing
>Let me explain it...
>It's...

giving up
>Pete, it is simply something one cannot lose

Pete
self-righteous and proud
>Well I just did!

James
>Alright then:

sits down
>Let's go through this very carefully
>Now, just start by telling me:
>How do you know you've lost it?

Pete
thinks
>I can't find it.

James
>That's no use.
>You have to tell me exactly what happened.

Pete
thinks
>Well ...
>Nothing really.

James
>There you are.

Pete
>Yeah
points at James, self-righteous
>But that is exactly what losing your karma is
>all about:
>Nothing happens any-more.

James
>Well, not much has changed in your life then,
>has it?

Pete
getting emotional
>But I feel so ... empty without it - without any
>plan, I don't know how to live my life ...
>I just haven't got a clue what to do ...
points at James, recovering
>Do you see - that is again because I've lost
>my karma:
>I don't know what to do.

James
yawning, picks up any book
>Yes, well, I'd really like to help you, but...
changes his mind
>O alright then, if you're really in such trouble:
closes book
>I think I might have a solution!

Pete
>What is it?

James
generously

> Pete, you karma-loser:
> Would you like to have some of mine?

Pete
first glad, then contemplates, rejects offer

> Ah! – oh – eh ... o no
> No thanks.

James

> Well - that was your one lucky chance I'm
> afraid.
> Now you've lost it – again.

Pete

> I don't want to be lost.
> I want to find it.
> Where is it?

James

> It might still be there where you lost it.
> Where did you lose it?

Pete

> That's a good one...
> I think it was when I went to the harbour.
> I was going to take the ferry you see - but I
> missed it.
> So now its gone.

James

> The ferry.

Pete

> No, my karma.
> I should have been on that ship...
> But I'm not - and now everything, my whole
> life ... has stopped.

James

> Well, it might still be on the ferry then - you
> could get yourself a ship and chase it.

Pete

Isn't that expensive?
Will you lend me some cash?!

James
changes his mind for economic reasons

Alternatively, you could ...
Start a search party

Pete

Yeah that's a great idea!
How do I do that?

James

Now, first of all:
We need to know what we're looking for.
So tell me, what does your karma look like?

Pete
thinks

Don't know –
optionally looks at the audience
Do <u>you</u> know what <u>your</u> karma looks like?

Enter Chuck looking at his mobile

Pete

Hi Chuck, you've come just at the right time,
you can definitely help me.

Chuck

Nope.
starts to leave again

Pete

O come on, I'm in deep trouble!

James
to Chuck

I'll tell you something:
He's actually lost his karma.

Pete
to Chuck

Yeah, stupid uh.
Chuck
Surely you have made a copy of it.
Pete stuns
You should make a copy of everything.
Anything important: – you should back it up.
If you haven't backed up your karma...

Chuck shakes his head, exits

Pete
Oh no! I don't have a copy!
I didn't bag it up!
I should have copied my karma - why hadn't I
thought of that?
broken
I'm lost,
It's the end!
James
My dear fellow, stop sobbing, just don't take it
too personally.
Take it more objectively - or better still:
scientifically!
Yes, dive into modern science - and do a
workshop.
A workshop on ... on reincarnation.
That will bring you to your past karma.
You really have to regress, dear man...
stands and closes his eyes, with his mouth open
Pete
stares at James
Workshop?
De-incarnation? Regress?
What is all that?
Is that going to work?
James, that is all too complicated for me.

Isn't there an easier way?
Wake up!

James
What?

I had this strange vision just now:
About someone who had no sausage left in
the fridge ...
And then suddenly an old piece appeared.
From behind the garlic tofu.
Pete
Karmic tofu?
What are you talking about?
Are you saying my karma is a sausage?
James
But none left ... in the fridge.
Pete
So when I think I don't have any karma – an
old sausage pops up?
James
From behind the garlic tofu, yes.
An old piece suddenly appears.
Pete
From the past?
I should find some old past karma,
somewhere, somehow?
And nick it?
James
You'd have to make sure its not overdue
though.
Or is karma always overdue?

Anyway - it sounds a bit weird, but it would
suit you though.

Pete

To be weird or not to be weird – that is not the
question.
If I can get my karma back doing this, then I
will try it out – right now.

starts to exit

I wonder where I will end up, going back ... to
my past ...
What is it? Where is it?
Who is it?
What does it look like?
I hope it'll be fun ...

exit Pete

*James searches in his books, mumbling "garlic
tofu"*

end of scene

SCENE 2

Scene – exterior, dark mood, a bench

Pete, later a Cube, Ex, the Mediator.
Ex: optionally loud, chewing bubble gum, wearing
riding boots, having a kind of whip.

Speaker:
> There is no port,
> there is nowhere to go
> only the deepening black
> darkening still blacker
> upon the soundless, ungurgling flood
> darkness at one with darkness,
> up and down and sideways utterly dark,
> so there is no direction any more
> and the little ship is there;
> yet she is gone.
> She is not seen,
> for there is nothing to see her by.
> She is gone! gone! and yet
>
> ...
> somewhere she is there.

Enter Pete

Pete
> I'm not sure...
> Do I really need to get back to my past?
> To get a piece of ... of what?

Sits down on the bench
> I don't even know where it is, my past...
> Or how to get there.

Enter a Cube walking by

Pete

> Hey you!
> How do I get back?
> Tell me how to get there.

Cube

stands, closes his eyes, speaks slowly

> To get
> your bag
> And find
> the way
> Await
> the Reign

Pete

> What?
> Waiting? - in the rain?
> Are you daft?
> I'll get wet.

Cube

> Prepare
> yourself
> If not
> too late
>
> ...

Enter Ex, who chases the Cube away, exit Cube

Ex

slowly

> Now look what we have here...
> A rotten piece of Revoltum Extinctum in full
> decay.

Pete

> O hell – it's my ex!

Ex

> Axe? Your axe?

Forgotten my name?

...

"Hell" – will do then

Pete

O! Eh ... alright, hi, eh, Hell, how are you?
I myself am in a bit of trouble you see...
So I wondered, if you could ....

Ex

looks in Pete's eyes

You!
Are waste –
Not even worth the bag you're in.
Get out.
And get lost.

Pete

looks in Pearl's eyes

I can't.
I'm already in, you see –
And also lost...
Lost my karma you see.
Do you have some to spare?
Just an old peace, you know.
Like from behind the garlic-tofu.

Ex

Karmic tofu?
You need a shrink you do
It's the old story, isn't it – clinically insane,
again, just like before.
Don't you remember?
Do you have any idea of what you've done?

...

You <u>left</u> me

whips Pete

Pete

What?

You left me!
Me you left.
Left me, you...

Ex

Right.
I was your luck – no idea how you found it
...and then you lost it!
You're just another loser.
I managed to lose you –
And then: I found this:
Mr. Fake in person:

Ex whips something, then enter Mediator

Ex: proudly, showing off
This is Ono.
He is a Mediator.
You'll never know what spit on you
whips the Mediator
Mediator
slimy, to Pete
How are we today?
Pete

...
Don't know ... lost...
Don't know
Mediator
Excellent answer - and even more excellent,
compliant with the art of mediation, one would
proceed in the following manner...
Pete has no power to resist, imitates Mediator
Smile, bend to the side, say: excellent
question, I am glad you asked, in a so
tolerant, so peaceful manner, that I would
answer with the same inclination, avoiding
any dogmatic or decisive scent and provide

you with an easily understandable and overall positive:

...
YES
Pete

...
You're bonkers
Totally

...
imitates the mediator
YES
Mediator
Excellent

Ex starts whipping the Mediator off the stage, he exits

Pete
imitating Mediator, including whipping
"Excellent"
"YES"
but Ex is still there
Ex
Can't ever say no, can you?
Pete
Do you want me to contradict your Fake then?
Ono? Is that what you want?
Against your friend?
Ex
Your friend, my friend, friends, you, me, axe, hell!
Pete
You're different, you've - changed ...
Or were you always - like this?
Ex
Dis-like? Chained?

You have to make up your mind, Petty:
It's up to you:
Change - or - chains.

Pete

"Excellent"
"YES"
What was her name again? - nah, lost it...
I'm losing everything now –
My.. Hell,
My karma,
My self...
monologue, optionally to the audience
Am I being selfish?
Wanting my own karma...
It's not that I am picky – but would not want
someone else's.
Simply just a bit of my own.
Not wanting it would be like suicide.

...

I'm getting tired of this...
sits down
Didn't know karma is so complicated.
I bet only experts know all the details.

*The same Cube enters and walks the same way as
before but now in the other direction, Pete
watches the Cube go by*

Maybe I should do that workshop after all.
Pete lies down on the bench
"You have to regress dear man" that's what
James said
No garlic-tofu any more.
This time it's for real:

A "De-incarnation workshop"...

...
"D-day"... here I come
falls asleep, lights fade

end of scene

SCENE 3

*Pete lies in the same place of the stage on a kind
of bed, James stands at his feet, Chuck at his
head, the whole scenery (dress, props) is ancient
Egyptian, Chuck reads from a book or sheet an
excerpt from the Egyptian book of the dead.*

Later Cubes, Butler

Chuck

> Homage to you, O ye gods who live in your
> hall Of Right and Truth.
>
> ...
>
> I have come unto you; I have committed no
> faults; I have not sinned; I have done no evil; I
> have accused no man falsely; therefore let
> nothing be done against me.
> I live in right and truth, and I feed my heart
> upon right and truth. That which men have
> bidden I have done, and the gods are satisfied
> thereat.
> I have pacified the god, for I have done his
> will.

*Looking at Pete, nothing happens, proceeding after
a short while, more intense*

> I have given bread unto the hungry and water
> unto those who thirst, clothing unto the naked,
> and a boat unto the shipwrecked mariner.
> I have made holy offerings unto the gods; and
> I have given meals of the tomb to the sainted
> dead.
> O, then, deliver ye me, and protect me;
> accuse me not before the great god.
> I am pure of mouth, and I am pure of hands.
> May those who see me say:

'Come in peace, come in peace.'

Chuck
	Nothing...
	Nothing's happening.
James
	That's normal.
	Let's just wait a while longer.

Chuck
	Do you think he's fallen asleep?
James
	Well...
	Speaking from a vast amount of experience
	on this subject, I have to say, falling asleep is
	one of the greatest of dangers here.
Chuck

	Is he still breathing??
	I'm not sure, James.
	What if we've done the wrong thing...
James
	Relax, we've done nothing wrong.
	In fact, we've done nothing at all.
Chuck
	I'm getting nervous.

	We'll both go to jail, you know, for doing this –
	or not doing it...
	They'll lock us up for ever!
James
	You're starting to scare me.
Chuck
	What do we do now?
James
	I don't know.

Perhaps we should quietly leave, and pretend
we never knew him.

Chuck
repeats

O, ... protect me; accuse me not ...
'Come in peace, come in peace.'

silence
then Pete slowly rises the upper part of his body,
similarly Pearl comes from the back of the centre-
stage slowly walking towards Pete

James & Chuck
looking at Pete

O shit!

as Pete starts to speak, Pearl moves backwards and
exits

Pete

Got you there!
You two were really scared weren't you guys?
...
Do you really believe this could ever actually
work?
How should this bring me back – to anything?
I can't get back to any past using some silly
text and improbable props.

Chuck
strong

No-body accuses me of being a bad prop...
Least of all a dead duck - last chance lost,
Dodo; you've just died out.
Back to nowhere is where you go from here -
I'll send you the bill

starts to work on his phone
James stands with his eyes closed and mouth open

Pete
the general mood is getting more aggressive

You stupid spiritists!
I was never in Egypt.

I didn't even make it to Spain.
Missed the Ferry, remember?
Where's my karma?
Does anybody see any karma here?

And what is <u>he</u> doing?
He looks like a path finder.
Why is he not a karma finder?

Chuck

Shut up.

Pete

He's just standing there doing nothing.
How long will he keep on doing this?

Chuck

Mute yourself.

Pete

Do you think he's ill? - or just being lazy as
usual?

Chuck
whispers

Don't you get it?
He is meditating.

Pete
loud

<u>Meditating</u>!?
Why doesn't he do something useful!
James puts his fingers in his ears, Pete tries to shout in James's ear
Like finding my karma?

Chuck

You are obsessed.
Get a life, get out of the picture and dissolve.

Pete

You are talking about <u>my life</u>!
What do <u>you</u> know about it?
    ...

Wait a minute ... perhaps you do – did you
steal my karma?
<u>Thief</u>!

James

Thou shalt not steal.
Steal not.

Pete

I thought you were asleep ...
What are you doing?

James

Await
the Reign
To find
the way

*James and Chuck start to exit into separate exits
left and right, Pete looks at them, unsure*

Pete

Hey - where are you two going?
What is this?
Is this a karmic thing?

...
Should I be in it then?
Do I have some – left – still – or not...?
Why are you going?
Don't leave me here.
Stay!
Stay please...
insecure, cuddles up front stage
...help...

*enter Pearl, comes in behind Pete,
she has a magic wand; she hands over a raincoat
with a label in it,
then speaking slowly, warm and clear*

Pearl

        Go on

        ...

        Go in

Pete puts on the coat

        ...

        Go

exit Pearl
the scene changes
enter four or more Cubes
Pete gets up, turns around

Cube

        Do you seek the Reign?

Pete

irritated

        What do you mean: seek the rain?
        Do you think I'm daft?
        Seek the rain - seek the rain ...
        Well...
        Perhaps...

Cube

        He is not one of us.

Cube

        Whose he is?

Pete

        I want to learn how to meditate,
        and then do a masters on it,
        and get a life and so on, you know.

Cube

        Definitely...

Cube

        Not us.

the cubes now form a square around Pete

Cube
		Come in.
Pete does not move, waits a moment
Pete
		Am I in, now?
Cube
		He is learning.
Cube
		You will be treated ...
Cube
		In accordance ...
Cube
		With your garments.
Pete
		What do you mean, treated?
		Like a massage?
		Should I lie down?
		I didn't bring a mat - or a pyjama or anything.
Cube
		We do not meditate lying down.
Cube
		Nor sitting down.
Cube
		We do ...
all Cubes
		Stand.

*all Cubes close their eyes, stand with their
mouths open; Pete has a closer look at them, then
tries it out himself (eyes closed, mouth open), at
some point he falls over, lights go out.
Pete stays on the stage in the same position until
the lights come up again.*

*the scene now has a kind of portal-like entrance,
after going through, Pete will be nearer to the
audience.*

Pete

Where am I?
O - hi there.
Who are you?

Butler

extremely friendly

Good evening Sir.
Can I take your coat please Sir?

Pete

assertive

Nah, don't bother, I'll keep it.

Butler

Can I take your coat please Sir?

Pete

What's your problem?
I might need it on the other side.
Never know what the weather is like over
there.

...
It might rain!

Butler

Couldn't agree more Sir
Very wise, if I may say so.
Now can I have your coat please?

Pete

I can go through as I like, you silly twit.
Nobody's gonna stop me from going in ...

*Pete shows how easily he might go through the
portal,
but never really does cross the entrance*

Pete

See?
I can do anything I like

Butler

> Certainly Sir.
>
> ...
> Your coat Sir?

Pete

> You don't seem to get it.
> My coat is a no go.

contradicting his words, Pete hands over his coat,
goes through the portal, stumbles, falls;
Butler steps in afterwards,
inspects the coat with changed voice and attitude,
outraged, bending over Pete

Butler

> Why couldn't you have just handed it over to
> me? What's the fuzz about giving your coat to
> me? Not too much to ask is it?
> Well is it? ...
> Lost you voice have you?

Pete

> I just thought...

Butler interrupts

Butler

> Nonono -not you, this is about <u>me</u>, for once.
> I stand there all the time waiting for you to
> hand over your coat, but you don't want that,
> do you? Do you know what it's like? Do you
> have any idea? Time after time, begging,
> pleading, begging again, having to crawl,
> smile ...
> And for what?
> For a ...

inspects the coat, flabbergasted

> O no, what is this?

Pete

> Well ...

Butler

You didn't really, did you?
You must be joking.
What on Earth do you want with this?

Pete

I... you....

Butler

O boy, I hope you're not serious.

Butler steps back across the portal again with the coat, changes back his voice and attitude

Butler

Enjoy your evening, Sir.

exit Butler with the coat

Pete, now front stage, speaks, optionally to the audience

Pete

That wasn't too bad was it?
I bet: no one has gotten as far as I have.
I must be miles ahead of every one else.

enter Pearl, wearing Pete's coat, walking up to him

Pete becomes ever more unsure

Pete
slowly

Holy shit, what's that?

Pearl
imitating Pete in reverse order, slowly

Shit hole, that's what.

Pete

That's not funny.

Pearl
prodding with her magic wand

You're not.

34

Pete
> What?

Pearl
> Joking?

Pete
> I don't like this.

Pearl
> Dislike, do you?

Pete
> I don't like you.

Pearl
> Like you, don't I?

Pete
> Who are you?
> What are you doing here?
> What am I doing here?
> Where am I?
> Who am I?
> This is getting on my nerves

Pearl
closing in on Pete
> I am on your nerves.
> I am in your blood.
> I am on you.

Pete
intimidated, desperate
> I want my coat back please.
> Give me my coat ...

Pearl
> ...back?
> To where we were?

Pete
> We?
> Me?
> You!

You, wearing my coat ...
You're a thief!

Pearl
strong

This coat has been lost.
Get a new coat.

Pete

That's not funny at all.

Pearl

Funny seek you?
I truth.

Pete

Truth?
What is that, truth?

Pearl
it is unclear if she is serious or not

Am I true?
To you?
Am I your friend?
You?
My friend?
Friends?

*Pearl offers her hand, Pete starts offering his,
she grabs it and starts arm wrestling, lights out,
or optionally with flash light while wrestling.*

end of scene

SCENE 4

Speaker

> The grim frost is at hand,
> when the apples will fall
> thick, almost thund'rous,
> on the hardened earth.
> And death is on the air
> like a smell
> of ashes!
> Ah! can't you smell it?

Enter Pete and James, talking

Pete

> ... and now I've also lost my coat!
> How do you like that?
> Not just my karma – or is that karma?

James

> Somebody might have run off with it.

Pete

> With my coat?
> Now that you mention it, I had this weird
> vision of a kind of portal ...

James
interrupting

> No, with your karma ...
> Come to think of it:

He'll be living your life then.

Pete

That's gonna be a big laugh for him.
He'll never know what hit him.

James

Or he is a she ...
Or a dog has eaten a part of it ...
Or something ...

Pete
interrupting

You're getting off track – I want my karma all
for myself.
I want the door-bell to ring and the delivery
man hands over my karma – something like
that ...
Otherwise I'm lost ... lost ...

James

My dear fellow, please don't be lost.
Do try and find yourself.

Pete

Yeah, sure, find myself.
Like going to the Lost & Found department
and having myself returned – to me.

James

Not such a bad idea actually.
Wouldn't you think so?
Just try your luck there - and see if your karma
has been found...
You have lost it already! - so that is a good
start.

Pete

Fantastic, yes, come on, let's go!

James

I say, do you really think that someone would
take the trouble to bring it to Lost & Found?

38

Well, I have to admit, if they did find it, they
probably would not want keep it...

Pete

What are you waiting for?
Come on!
I'm off!

Office-clerk
*practising his text from a piece of paper in case
someone would enter, rocking back and forth*

I ... am afraid ... we have ... no such items ... at
the moment ... Sir
I ... am afraid ... we have ... no such items ... at
the moment ... Sir
I ... am afraid ... we have ... no such items ... at
the moment ... Sir

*Enter Pete and James,
Office-clerk gets nervous*

Pete

Well, at least we've found the office, that's
something.
It's worth the try.
to the Office-clerk
Hi there!
Do you have any karma here?
I've lost mine, you see, can't find it.

Office-clerk
having difficulties producing his text
I ... am afraid ... we have...

Pete
interrupting
Did you say you have?

Office-clerk
	I ... am afraid ...
James
interrupting
	He says he's afraid.
Office-clerk
	I ...
James
soothing
	Let's not bother him any-more.
	Looks to me like a case of burn-out ...
Office-clerk
	I ... I ... I ....
collapses and disappears behind the counter
James
	O dear, burned down ...
Office-clerk reappears and puts a plastic bag for dog-waste with soft content on the counter
Pete
	O shit!
James
	You might say that again ...
inspects the bag
	Could well be yours I suppose.
	Does your karma smell like this?
Pete
inspects the bag
	It stinks ...
to the Office-clerk
	Are you sure this is all you have?
Office-clerk
	I ... I ... I ....

Enter Chuck

Chuck
	What's that smell?

James
points at the bag
>It's his karma I'm afraid.

Chuck
sees the bag
>Wow, so that is what karma looks like!
>Never seen it before!

makes selfies with the bag, the Office-clerk joins in
Chuck shows the pictures to James

James
looking at the photos
>Doesn't look very appetizing.

Chuck
shows pictures to Pete
>You need to get something more edible than that.
>Something like – garlic-tofu.

Pete
>Edible?
>Appetizing?
>That's disgusting!

Chuck
>I suppose you're right – I don't think I would like to devour my karma, come to think of it.
>Especially if the substance is not edible...

prods the bag
>It's the wrong stuff.
>It's too soft, you see.
>You'll need to tune it up, and make proper hard-ware out of it.

Pete
>It can't be the wrong stuff - this is this my karma.
>Or is my karma wrong?
>Doesn't look like it – does it?
>...

I'm confused.
James
>I'll tell you, the best thing to do, is simply to get back to where you were ...
>Back to the past, then you know what you have.
>That is where I always go.

James exits

Chuck
>Getting back to where you were?
>Getting nowhere you mean – that's no use.
>Why don't you listen to me?
>It is like I said: better try it the hard way.
>Take your stuff and go to the hard-ware store.
Shows something on his phone
>That's where to go to tune it up.
>They can do so much these days, it's the thing of the future.
Pete
stares at his bag
>Do you really think tuning up a doggy bag is the thing to do?
Chuck
>Come <u>on</u>!

Chuck tries in vain to make Pete move by working on his mobile, then exits

Pete stands waiting, looking at his bag all the time, holding it in front of his eyes

enter Pearl – while she speaks, Pete tries to listen to the bag

Pearl
>Fully bagged thy karma lies
>Of this bag a scent evades
>From those pearls that were thy cries
>Nothing of this that does fade
>But does suffer a time-change
>Into something rich and strange

lights slowly fade

end of scene

SCENE 5

Speaker

>Now launch the small ship,
now as the body dies
and life departs,
launch out, the fragile soul
in the fragile ship of courage,
the ark of faith
with its store of food
and little cooking pans
and change of clothes,
upon the flood's black waste
upon the waters of the end
upon the sea of death,
where still we sail
darkly, for we cannot steer,
...
and have no port.

Enter Chuck and Pete

Chuck

>Here we have it:
– this is where it all happens:
Pete, just believe in the hard way and let the
system-manager make your karma great
again

Pete and Chuck enter the store

Pete

>Hi there!

I have had a kind of a karma crash.
And I haven't made a copy.
Didn't bag it up, you know.
But I have some left overs, you see.
shows the doggy bag
Can you remake my karma with this?
System-manager
inspects the bag
This looks like soft stuff.
Did you code it yourself?
Chuck
He did – might be a bit dodgy.
System-manager
Need to make hard-ware out of it.
Provided it be free of bugs.
That will cost ... quite a byte – and requires a
new operating system.
Pete
confused
Bugs, operating? I don't want to be operated
on, not even on my bag – you get it?
Chuck
lecturing to Pete
Take it easy, I know this, this is binary-speak.
Don't forget: he – is a System-manager.
It'll all be alright.
But what he's really saying basically means:
shakes his head
It'll cost you a fortune.
Pete
to the system-manager
Well ...you know...
I am a little short on cash right now...
But I think I will win the lottery soon - should
be in my karma you see: to be fortunate at the
right moment.

Just repair it and you'll see it.
I'll let you have half of it – of the lottery thing I
mean.
System-manager
How many bits will that bring?
Pete
does not understand, makes something up
Bits?
Yeah, loads of bits and pieces.
To make up a whole new karmic copy.
That'll do it.
System-manager
puts the bag on the scanner
Right then.
This is your karma?
Pete
Yep.
System-manager
Your name.
Pete
Me.
System-manager
Password.
Pete
outraged
Password?
It's a bag for dog-shit.
It doesn't have a password!
System-manager
It won't run, anyway.
It's in the wrong format.
It's incompatible.
Pete
confused
Incompatible?
With what?

System-manager
>   With your life.
Pete
irritated
>   Listen Sys-co, I have lost my karma, this is all
>   I have left, I am lost, don't tell me I can't live
>   this karma!
System-manager
the system produces sounds, the System-manager
looks worried on his system
>   Have you run a virus check on this?
puts on a mask
>   Do you feel ill?
>   Infected?
>   Contagious?
Pete
still irritated
>   Listen mister Sys-teen.
>   Use your last brain cell.
>   If I don't have any karma, I cannot make
>   anybody ill, can I?
System-manager anxiously starts taking pills and
injects himself
Pete takes the bag and leaves the store in anger,
Chuck follows
Pete
>   Incompatible!
>   That's what Systole the Great said.
>   What does <u>he</u> know about it?
>
>   ...
>   And what do I know about it?
>   Is this really my karma?
>   How can I find out?
>   What I'm supposed to do?
>   Its the same problem all the time, you know,
>   trying to find my karma.
>
>   ...

In fact, it has to be my karma to find my karma
– otherwise I cannot find it ...
But at the moment I don't have any, so I will
never be able to find it

...
Its a dead end.

Chuck

Couldn't you just pretend to have karma?

Pete

What do you mean?

Chuck

Like injecting yourself with a terrible disease.

Pete

And then what?

Chuck

Well, then when you're ill you say – oh I'm ill,
must be karmic, bad karma in the past, or
something like that.

Pete

And then what?

Chuck

Nothing.
Its just pretend.
It is what everybody does all the time – play
pretend.

Pete

But it's not real, nothing is changed, its no
use.

Chuck

I'm only trying to help.

Pete

Its more like pretending to help.

Chuck

Your getting philosophical – whom have you
been reading?

Pete

I don't read people.
I read books – sometimes.

...
That reminds me - of James.
Perhaps I should do what he said - go back.
To the old stuff
To where I was ...
Start again, from the beginning.
Having useless infantile discussions while
gathering dust, as always ...

...
I'm running out of options.
lights slowly fade
I don't want to fade away...

End of scene

SCENE 6

*James and Pete are on stage, Pete looks depressed
later Chuck and Pearl*

*Speaker optionally walks around on the stage this
time, speaking slowly, directing the words towards
Pete*

Speaker
>   Now, if you want to stay
>   Not have to fade away
>
>   ...
>   That, what will keep you here
>   So you will you have no fear
>
>   ...
>   Is just what karma feeds
>   Is lots of evil deeds
>
>   ...
>   And with such guilt galore
>   You'll have to fear no more
>
>   ...
>   But if there's not enough
>   Make sure that things get rough
>
>   ...
>   Want some?
>   Get some!
>   Slay one.

James
>   Have you tried posting that you've lost it?
>   Perhaps someone came across it, and does
>   not know what it is.

Pete

I don't know what it is myself.

James

There, you see ...
But they might ask a reward.
Or perhaps not, ... is it valuable?

Pete

Don't know.

...

Perhaps it is one of those things that's run out
of credit.

...

Hey wait a minute:
Maybe I only need to top it up!

James

Topping it up – sounds like a sound idea.
What would you like to top it up with?

Pete

Well ...
Just some goodies, you know like good deeds
and stuff.
Yeah I'll be like Father Theresa or Saint
French.
You know: giving everything away.
To the poor.

James

But you've just lost it.
Your karma.
Your life.
Everything.
Its gone, pal.
You're done.

Pete

O my God!

Chuck
>> Found some karma?
looks at his mobile, worried
>> How about paying my bills?
James
>> He's still in the process of searching.
Chuck
>> For money, I'm sure.
James
>> Not quite, he's still looking for his karma I'm afraid.
Chuck
looks at Pete
>> Look at him:
>> What karma should that have?
>> I bet its simply over.
Pete
>> What do you mean, over?
Chuck
>> That there is no more.
>> You're finished.
Pete
>> But then I have to die!
Chuck
>> Don't take it personally.
looks at his device
Chuck
>> Got to go.

Exit Chuck

Pearl enters, appears to Pete only, James does not notice

Pete

> O no, not you again ...
> Are you always with me?
> There where I am?

Pearl

> Are <u>you</u>?

Pete

> No: <u>you</u>, are <u>you</u>?

Pearl

> Are you there?

Pete

> You really make me – you – I don't even know
> your name ...

Pearl

> You do.

Pete

> Me?

Pearl

> <u>YES</u>

exit Pearl

Pete

> What was that all about?
> Was that good or bad?
> ...
> James, I really must find a way to top it up
> somewhere.
> I don't want to die.
> You'll give me a last chance, won't you?

James

> Well – the last thing I can think of...
> But I'm not sure if I should mention it ...

Pete
optionally kneels

O come on, just put every card on the table,
Jimmy!
Consider this to be a karmic situation.
Something you simply cannot avoid.

James

Well alright then:
Isn't there this story with this man, what's his
name ...

*James and Pete optionally come up with names of
locals known to the audience*

James

Wait, I got it: it was Faust!
I mean, you could do the same thing and
simply:
Try the devil.

Pete
upset

The devil?

James
jolly

Yes - why not just give it a try?

Pete

Which devil do you mean?

James

Hey:
The wrong one of course.

Pete

Isn't that dangerous?
I mean: calling up the devil...
That could be lethal.

...

Maybe I should text him first.
Do you have his number?

James

Have his number? Me?
What do you think?

Chuck
looking around

This stupid thing got me right back to where I
started.

James
to Pete, pointing at Chuck

<u>He</u> might.

to Chuck

I didn't do it.

Exit James

Chuck

What's the matter with him?

Pete

O – he was just trying to be helpful.
I think.
Can I use your mobile?

Chuck

<u>My</u> mobile?

Laughs

You?
No way teddy boy.
You're bad luck.
You're a no-go.
You're dead.
You're extinct.

looking at his device

And broke.

*Exit Chuck, in the process Pete finds a way to get
a hold of Chuck's mobile*

Pete
working on the device

Now who was it?
John Smith? – no.
optionally tries some local names known to the audience
Pete

What's this: any-body? - no.
No-body? – OK, I'll try that one.
What shall I write?
Contemplates, then the phone rings, Pete takes the call

Me speaking.

...

Who's that?...
How did you know I wanted ...?
What do you mean: - before it is too late? ...
Do you know who I am? ...
No ... who are you?
drops the phone accidentally, picks it up, tries it out, listens

Dead. It's dead.
Reads on the mobile

Hey, wait a minute.
There is a message.
What's this?
Reads, slowly

Now, if you want to stay
Not have to fade away

...

That, what will keep you here
So you will you have no fear

...

Is just what karma feeds
Is: lots of evil deeds

...

And with such guilt galore
You'll have to fear no more

...

But if there's not enough
Make sure that things get rough

...
Want some?
Get some!
Slay one.

Pearl

Have you built your ship of death?
O build your ship of death!

Pete

What is going on here?
What is this?

...
Build a death ship?
Slay someone?

...
And that should give me karma?
I don't want to die.

*Mood, lights/music and so change
enter James, Chuck, Pearl and all other available
actors moving chaotically around the stage
Pete finds a weapon; confused, he points the
weapon at different persons, eventually attacks
Pearl at some part of her body – just before he
actually would hit Pearl, lights black-out (or
optionally instead: a flash with actors freezing)*

end of scene

SCENE 7

Speaker
optionally walking through the audience as before
> And everything is gone,
> the body is gone
> completely under, gone, entirely gone.
> The upper darkness is heavy as the lower,
> between them the little ship
> is gone
> she is gone.
> It is the end,
> it is oblivion.

Enter Chuck, starts searching everywhere

James
> O, do come in Chuck, how are we today?
>
> ...
> What are you looking for?
> Have you lost something?

Chuck
> I can't believe it.
> I have actually lost .... lost my mobile!

sits down, depressed
> You've got to help me James, help me!

James
> Chuck, calm down.
> Now let me explain this to you:
> One <u>does</u> loose ones mobile all the time.
> It's a common thing – it's actually becoming a
> tradition.
>
> ...

But surely you have made a back-up of it.
One should always make a copy of
everything, you know.

Chuck

Copy? A copy?
Who cares about a copy?
I want the real thing and I want it now!

James

Oh well...
Just don't worry about it.
It's only your mobile.

Chuck

Only my mobile?!
You are talking about my life, my everything...
This is the end!

Shakes James

I am lost!

James

Chuck, do calm down now.

...

Perhaps Pete knows what to do.
He is an experienced loser ... if you know what
I mean.

Enter Pete and Pearl from left and right
Pete has an additional bandage, there where he
tried to attack Pearl, and a doggy bag with
garlic-tofu
Pearl has some unused bandage with her, ready to
apply

James

What happened to you my dear fellow?
Must have found some karma.
Or has it found you?

Pete

I don't know.

60

                I haven't got a clue.
                I wish I knew.
                What happened.
                I don't remember.
                Where this comes from.
Shows bandage
                Nor who done it.
                Who would do such a thing?
Pearl

                Was it me?
                I hope it wasn't me.
                Do you think it was me?
                Tell me it wasn't me.
Pete

                What?
James

                She does look somewhat guilty, I have to say.
Chuck
to James

                Yeah, now that you mention it.
                She must have stolen my mobile too!
to Pearl

                Where is it?
                Give it to me!
starts chasing Pearl
Pete

                Give...?
*Takes Chuck's mobile out of his pocket and holds
it up, at first unnoticed by Chuck*
                I give it up.
                I'll get on a ship.
                And sail away.
                Into oblivion.
Chuck

                Never mind oblivion.
                I have lost my mobile!

My life has come to an end ...

Pete

Here it is.
Found it – somewhere – by magic – if you
know what I mean.

Chuck

Wow! Great! You've given me back my life!
How can I thank you!

starts to work on his mobile

Pete

I'll think of something, don't you worry.

Chuck

O no - it does not work ... it's dead!
I'm dead again!

James

to himself

One into oblivion.
One dead.

...

Now what about me?

to Chuck

Say, Chuck, I was thinking ...
Do you think ... other people ... can they lose
their karma as well?

Chuck

You mean like losing a mobile phone?

Optionally to the audience

What is the difference between karma and a
mobile phone?

James

I wouldn't want to die like Pete.
Nothing personal.
Can anybody tell me what the symptoms are?

Shivers, as having a cold

And what I should do?
I don't feel very well ...

        Has that System-manager infected me?
Pearl
describes the situation
        It is getting cold here.
James
        What was that?
Looks around
        Cold?
        Now that you mention it – perhaps I only have
        a cold.
        I hope.
Pearl starts to wrap part of James in bandages
Chuck
        It <u>is</u> getting cold here ...
shivers
        What's wrong with the heating?
        Is it bugged?
        If I only could get my mobile to work ...
Pete
        Maybe if we eat something, it might warm us
        up.
        I have some left-overs.
inspects the bag he has with him
        I'm afraid I only have some old pieces of
        garlic-tofu...
Presents a doggy bag with tofu to Chuck
        Want some? - get some! - take one.
Chuck
takes a peace, eats
        Doesn't help.
*Pearl starts to wrap part of Chuck with the
bandage*
James
*Pete presents the bag to James, who does not take
anything*
        Ah - eh - no, no – no thanks.

Pete

> But there must be something we can do.
> ...
> Maybe we should get closer together.

Pete James Chuck cuddle up

Chuck
anxious

> Do you think this is it?
> Is this the end?
> It's not like I imagined it.
> They say it never is.
> It's unexpected.

James
shivering

> They say it's like going on a journey.
> Or taking a ship.
> To some unknown island.
> Sailing off into the sunset.
> Indefinitely.

Pete
feeling positively content

> I feel more like we're in a doggy bag!
> All together:
> Dark, smelly, brooding.

Pearl
clearly and slowly, imperative

> Time - to clean up!

Pete James Chuck, startled, look at Pearl

Chuck

> What is that?
> You scare me.

To James

> Who is this, anyway?

James

> I actually don't really know I'm afraid.
> Familiar to you, Pete?

Pete
        No?
        Yes?
looks at Pearl, dreamy
        Is it you again?
        What is it this time?
        What do you mean?
        What are you saying?
Contemplates, more awake
        Time to clean up

        ...
        Is this one of your riddles again?
        Cleaning up?

        ...
*optionally touched by Pearl's stick and
enlightened*
        That's it!
        Found it!
        That is exactly what I will do:
        I'm going to clean up!

        ...
        Taking care of people's doggy bags!
embraces Chuck and James
        I've found it!
        I'm in business.
        I'm starting up, finally.
James
        Now, seriously, found what?
        Your karma?
Chuck
        My money?
Pete
        Yes, no, I don't know
        It's all new, it's the new me,
        It's me!
Imitating the mediator

<u>YES</u>!
...
I can see it all happening:
I'm going to start my own business
Cleaning up doggy bags for other people.
What shall I call it?
I'll call it something like:
into the audience
"Clean Up Your Life – Incorporated"
James
You mean starting a business?
In this world as we have it?
Isn't that dangerous?
I would just stick with tradition.
Go back to how things were.
That is what I always do.

Chuck
moaning, childish
I just want my mobile to work.
I want the door-bell to ring and the delivery
man hands over my mobile, with the latest
apps – something like that.

Pete
happy day-dreaming
I can see it - written in gold:
"clean up your life"
...
Chuck, if it brings any money, I'll buy you a
mobile.
James, if it works, I'll write a book about it.
...
This is the new dawn.
Believe you me:
When your karma is lost, this is what you do:
Get yourself a new life.

Speaker
> Wait, there's the dawn,
> the cruel dawn of coming back to life
> out of oblivion.

Optionally all together
> And the little ship wings home,

> ...

> and the frail soul steps out,
> into the house again
> filling the heart with peace.

Pearl
in the mean time solemnly walking up to front stage, then joking

> Time to clean up!

END

A PLAYWRIGHT'S NOTES

I am not in favour of many stage directions –
basically, I would like to have none ... so feel free to
ignore them and do your own thing.

In fact, I am not particularly keen on written text at all
... do you think, I should just leave you with empty
pages and all the space you need to live your art?

If you still think you're seeing letters in black ink on
white paper, don't let them disturb you too much -
create your play, interpreting, improvising and
listening to that what some people think is
coincidence and chance.

Share your production with others.
Then clean up.
Time to clean up!
Or is it?

What happens next?
What about Pete and the others?
Where will they be in the years to come?

Do I see a Gecko, a CEO of a thriving bagging
service provider – not taking things too seriously
when it comes to the moral side of his enterprises?

His corruption of the karmic cleanse can leave Pearl
no other choice but to cross his path again, herself
having achieved the state of homelessness, and
drawing from that the impulse and power to enlighten

her former pupil.

And where is James? Is James? At all? In a cave,
being manipulated by a dark shadow of something
like a system-manager of the wrong.

While Chuck, on the other hand has flipped his bits
and has gone vegan, an activist, chewing carrots,
getting closer to Pearl, helping her out where
possible.

Or so it seems.
To me.

But perhaps, or surely, you see things differently.
Won't you?

So,
finally,
here they are,
the empty pages :